The English Concertina
ABSOLUTE BEGINNERS

Alex Wade and Dave Mallinson

Detailed tuition for the English concertina, designed to speed up the learning process.

Foreword by David Ledsam

I became aware of Alex Wade's concertina playing when judging a Rapper Sword Dance competition in Derby. Right from the first note I knew I was listening to a very special musician and player of the English Concertina. She played with touch, great speed and what was most important, driving rhythm. I awarded her full marks, which is generally unheard of in this competition.

Since then I heard her many times playing for dance or at sessions and I have remained as impressed as when I heard her first. She has a great musical ear and I am very pleased that Mally asked me to contribute to this excellent beginners English Concertina tutor.

Many learners of the English will be inspired by the playing of Alex, and this book will give them an invaluable start in their journey to becoming a player of this most beautiful and portable instrument, the English Concertina.

A soundtrack (DMPCD1301) has been prepared by Alex to accompany this book.
The recording is available from traditional music shops or direct from the publishers.

The English Concertina - Absolute Beginners   Alex Wade and Dave Mallinson
Alex Wade: Recording, fingering and technical information
Dave Mallinson: Design, tune arrangements, text, artwork and photography
Tune arrangements, tuition and text copyright © Dave Mallinson 2013

ISBN 978 1 899512 80 5
A catalogue in print record for this title is available from the British Library.

Acknowledgements
Technical proof reading: Alex Wade and Steve Wood
Grammatical proof reading: Steve Wood and Alistair Russell
Essay, English Concertina Tutor - The Basics: Ian Goodier
Thank you: Richard Harrison for help with photography and encouragement.
Thank you: Steve Wood, Alistair Anderson and Andy Day for invaluable comments and suggestions
which have had a massive influence on the shaping of this book.
Thank you: David Ledsam, Soar Valley Music, for permission to photograph front cover background concertina.
Thank you: Chris Algar, Barleycorn Concertinas, for permission to photograph front cover foreground concertina.

All rights reserved. No part of this book may be reproduced in any form whatsoever without prior written permission from the publisher, except for short extracts for reviews. This book is sold subject to the condition that it shall not, by way of trade or otherwise, be lent, re-sold or otherwise circulated without the publisher's prior consent, in any form of binding or cover other than that in which it is published.

It is illegal to photocopy any part of this book
Produced and published by **mally.com**
3 East View, Moorside, Cleckheaton, West Yorkshire, BD19 6LD, U.K.
Telephone: +44 (0)1274 876388
Email: mally@mally.com   Web: http://www.mally.com
Copyright © 2013 mally

A mally production

Introducing Music Basics for Squeezers

Printed music is a means of conveying musical messages from one person to another or from one person to many. It's simply a means of communication. It's very useful because receivers can accept the information at any pace they choose. Acquiring tunes from recordings can be laborious, especially to the unpractised ear. Some passages are often difficult to make out. No such problem with printed music; the information remains static for as long as necessary, it's clear, precise and can be accurately absorbed.

A melody is a series of sounds of varying pitch and length, and each sound is called a note. Printed music uses symbols to represent these notes. The shape tells us how long the note lasts, and its position on a grid of five parallel lines and four spaces denotes the pitch. This grid is called the stave, and each line and space has a name which is given to any note placed there.

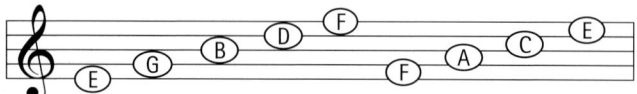

Notes are written on the lines and spaces, and also above and below the stave on small leger lines called leger lines. They are named after the first seven letters of the alphabet. When you get to G you start again at A. The symbol found at the beginning of each line of music is called a treble clef. It tells us that the names of the notes are as shown above. You only need to remember one to be able to find out the rest, and just to make it really simple, the notes in the spaces just happen to spell the word FACE, going from bottom to top.

For players of traditional music, music for the concertina always has a treble clef sign at the beginning of each line and a key signature consisting of one, two or three sharps. A sharp is represented by the symbol ♯. It raises the pitch of a note by one semitone, the smallest interval of musical pitch. When there is one sharp in the key signature, it is always placed on the F line. This tells us that all F notes have to be raised by one semitone to F sharp (F♯). One sharp indicates the key of G major. Here are the main notes of G major.

When a second sharp is added, it is placed on the C space, so now all F notes and C notes are raised by one semitone to F♯ and C♯. Two sharps in the key signature indicates the key of D major. These are the main notes of D major.

Three sharps indicates the key of A major. It is important to memorise where to find these notes on your instrument.

The shape of musical notes tells us how long they are to be sounded. The length of time a note is sounded is not an exact measurement of time, but a comparative amount of time in relation to the other notes. Here's how they relate to each other.

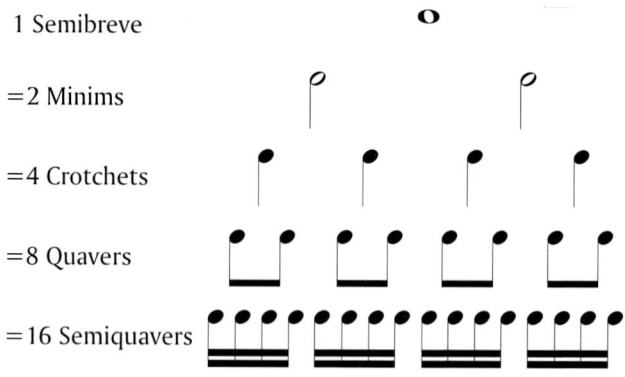

1 Semibreve
=2 Minims
=4 Crotchets
=8 Quavers
=16 Semiquavers

Quavers and semiquavers have the symbols ♪ and ♫ when they occur singly but are joined together when they occur in groups. For each note there is an equivalent symbol to indicate a period of silence. These symbols are called rests. Sometimes a note or a rest has a dot after it. This means that the note or rest is held for half as long again. Rests and their equivalent notes are shown below.

Music has a steady throb or pulse which you can clap along to. These pulses are called beats, some of which are stronger than others. The strong or accented beats occur at regular intervals forming the beats into groups of two, three or four. A piece of music is naturally divided into equal measures by these groups of beats which are known as bars. In order to show where these divisions come bar lines are placed across the stave in front of the accented notes. Each beat of a bar receives one count. In order to denote what type of beat grouping will present itself in a piece of music, a time signature is placed immediately after the key signature at the beginning of the piece. The top number denotes the number of counts per bar. The bottom number denotes the type of note that receives one count. 4 = ♩ (crotchet)   8 = ♪ (quaver). Thus:

2/4 means 2 crotchets to the bar
4/4 means 4 crotchets to the bar
3/4 means 3 crotchets to the bar
6/8 means 6 quavers to the bar

The symbol :|| means repeat from the symbol ||:, or if that symbol doesn't occur, repeat from the beginning.

This curved line ♩‿♩ joining two notes of the same pitch together is called a tie. It means the values of the two notes are added together and sounded as one.

The flat ♭ lowers a note by one semitone in pitch.

The natural ♮ restores a note to its original pitch.

Where these brackets |1. |2. occur, play the notes under 1. first time and the notes under 2. on the repeat.

The English Concertina Fingering Chart

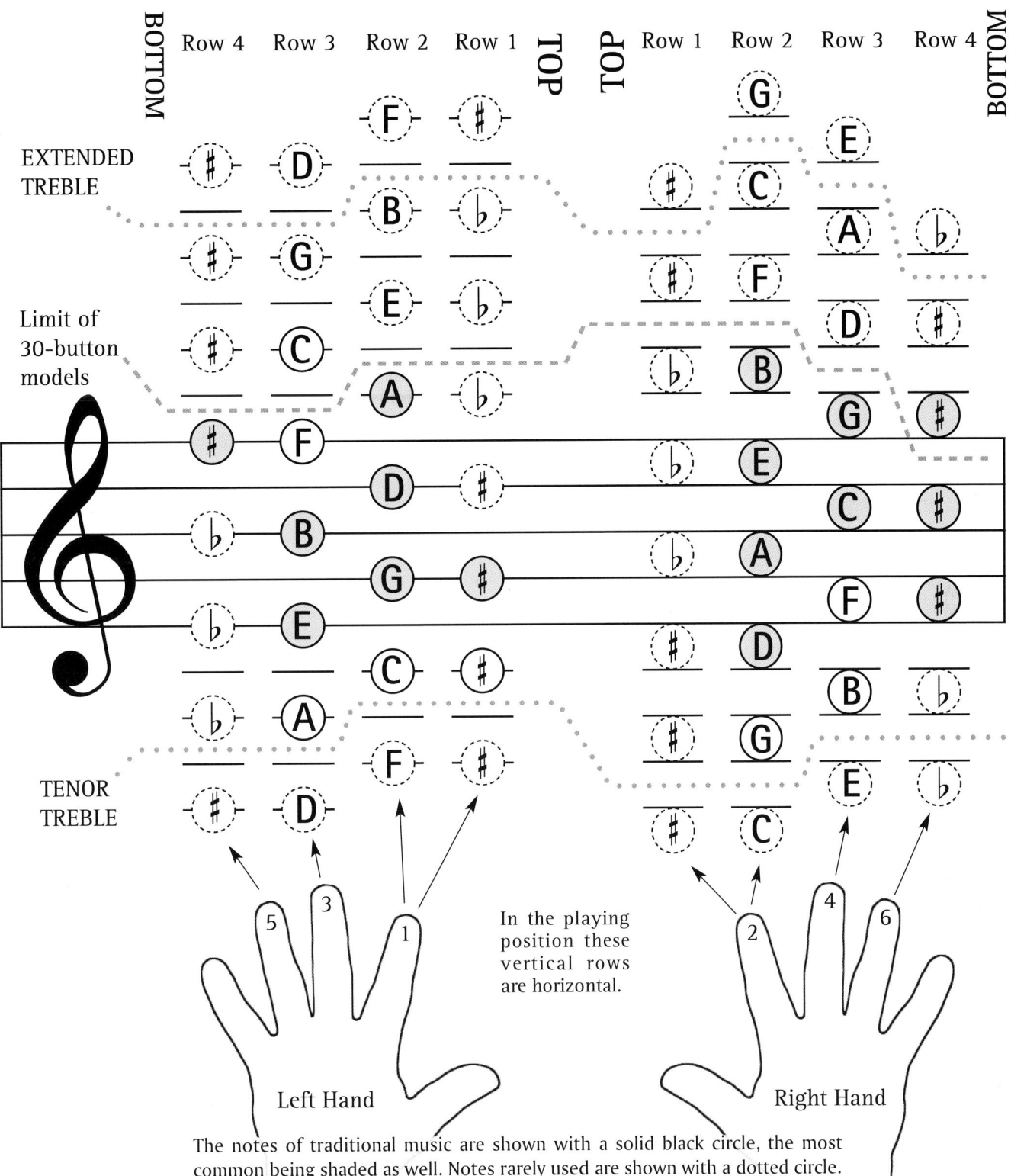

The notes of traditional music are shown with a solid black circle, the most common being shaded as well. Notes rarely used are shown with a dotted circle.

There are several different types of English concertina. The **Treble** with 48 buttons is the standard, it has the same range as the violin (called the fiddle in our world of traditional music). On the diagram above the notes of the treble are shown between the dotted lines. Treble instruments with 30 buttons are also available, the dashed line shows the limit of their range. The **Extended Treble** has 56 buttons, extending the musical range at the top end of the scale. The **Tenor Treble** has 56 buttons, extending the musical range at the bottom end to that of the viola. If your instrument is a tenor treble you must play one button further along to that shown in the note-layout diagrams. A few 64-button instruments were made which had the range of the extended treble and tenor treble combined. The **Baritone** is played exactly the same as the treble but sounds one octave lower. The **Piccolo** sounds one octave higher than the treble; they are very small and don't have many buttons but are treated exactly the same as treble instruments. **Bass** concertinas sound two octaves below the treble, although some only go down to C rather than the bottom G; many of them sound only in one direction, on the push of the bellows. All the different types have the same fingering system; middle rows play the C scale, outer rows play the sharps and flats. Learn a tune on one and you can play it on another.

The English Concertina Absolute Beginners

Introducing the English Concertina

The concertina is one of the free reed range of instruments. It's related to the harmonica, the bandoneon, the piano accordion, the button accordion and the melodeon. A free reed is a tongue of metal which is allowed to vibrate freely within a metal frame, usually called a plate. It doesn't strike against another object to produce the sound, unlike reeds in instruments such as clarinets, saxophones and bassoons. The reed is made to vibrate by forcing air to rush past using a bellows, or in the case of harmonicas, the lungs.

Concertinas were developed independently in England and Germany in the late 1820s. Many new developments and improvements were made in the 1830s. German-made instruments played a different note on each bellows direction, and when made and improved in England, became known as Anglo concertinas. Instruments originating in England became known as English concertinas, they had the same note on both bellows directions.

This book is concerned only with the English concertina. It was invented by Charles Wheatstone in 1829. Over many years he improved the design and layout. By the mid 1840s they were being manufactured in large quantities and their popularity soared. Concertina bands were formed and the instruments were much favoured by the Salvation Army who liked them for their portability and strident tone. In recent years, the English concertina has undergone a resurgence in popularity in Britain and America by becoming much favoured by players of traditional music.

Internally the English concertina is a complicated masterpiece of engineering, featuring a host of levers, springs and reeds. However, all this is hidden from view. From the outside, it's a very simple but often very beautiful object. It consists of a bellows attached to wooden ends with six, eight or twelve sides. Each end has four rows of studs (the buttons), a small leather strap (the thumb strap) and a metal plate (the finger rest). Some instruments have an extra stud on one side (the air button). The number of buttons can vary but the most common instruments have 48 or 56. Some instruments have only 30 buttons and a few have as many as 60. All these instruments are ideal for use with this book. Hopefully you own an English concertina and you are eager to learn to play some traditional music.

The buttons on the English concertina are arranged in rows, four on each side. Counting from nearest the thumb strap, the rows are numbered 1 to 4. The index finger is used to play buttons on rows 1 and 2, the middle finger is used to play buttons on row 3 and the ring finger plays buttons on row 4. The two middle rows play the same notes as the white piano keys; the outer rows play the same notes as the black keys. So any particular finger, of either hand, can easily be referred to they have been numbered, as shown on page 3. Fingers of the left hand have been given odd numbers and right-hand fingers have been allotted even numbers.

Bellows technique is a skill that can only be learned over time, and all players must develop their own personal style. There are various initial approaches. Rest the left-hand side of the instrument on your left leg and operate the bellows with your right arm. Rest the right-hand side on your right leg and operate the bellows with your left arm. Rest the whole instrument gently on one knee and operate the bellows with both arms. These are the standard beginners playing positions. Many experienced players prefer to play the instrument unsupported, allowing for a more dynamic style of playing. Some players, when playing standing, favour the use of a neck or shoulder strap to support the

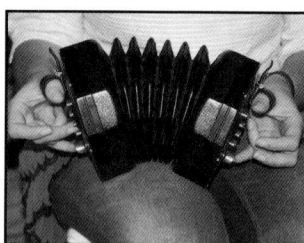

instrument. Alex favours the whole instrument on the knee approach, as shown here. However, it must be pointed out that if you adopt this style you could damage the bellows. If you allow the bellows to constantly rub against your clothes, they will eventually wear out. On the plus side, tapping out the beat with this leg creates an extra pulse in the music by making small air pressure changes. It's also worth pointing out that in the heyday of the English concertina, the Salvation Army tuition books recommended operating the bellows with the right arm.

OK, sit on a comfortable dining chair or stool; pick up your concertina and hold it with your thumbs through the straps (only up to the first joint is recommended) and your little fingers under the finger rests. This leaves the other three fingers of each hand free to operate the buttons. You might have to adjust the thumb straps so they are not causing pain but are tight enough to feel that you are fully

in control of the instrument. It will be immediately apparent that it is impossible to hold the instrument the wrong way round. Experiment with the different holding techniques outlined above. Find one that works for you, then you are ready to play.

Press any button and pull the bellows out to make a sound called a note. Now push the bellows in and play the same note. Repeat this several times, pressing various buttons to play several different notes, until you get the feel of the instrument. Push and pull the bellows evenly, keep the air pressure constant to play notes of equal volume. Throughout the book, symbols have been placed over the music to indicate where to push and pull the bellows; V = pull bellows, ⊓ = push bellows. Never move the bellows without pressing one or more buttons or the air button, as this could seriously damage your instrument. If you have an air button, use it to close the bellows after playing; if not, hold down several buttons and gently close the bellows, making as little sound as possible.

It isn't necessary to practise the concertina for hours in order to create a nice sound. Instruments such as trumpet, flute and violin require hours of work just to acquire the skill to blow or bow a note correctly. With instruments such as guitar and banjo you have the irksome task of tuning before you start. Concertina players are off to a flying start; just press, squeeze and play.

Introducing the Key of C Major

Little Brown Jug

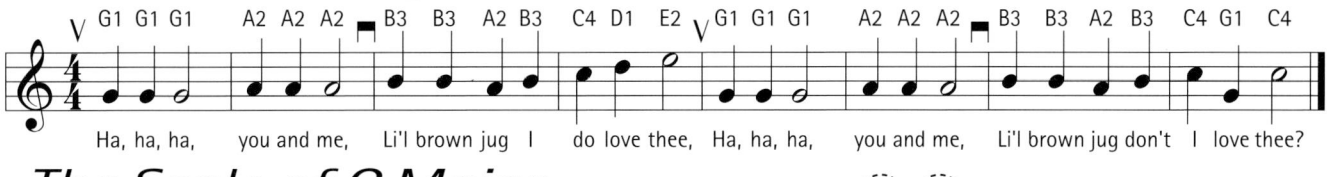

The Scale of C Major

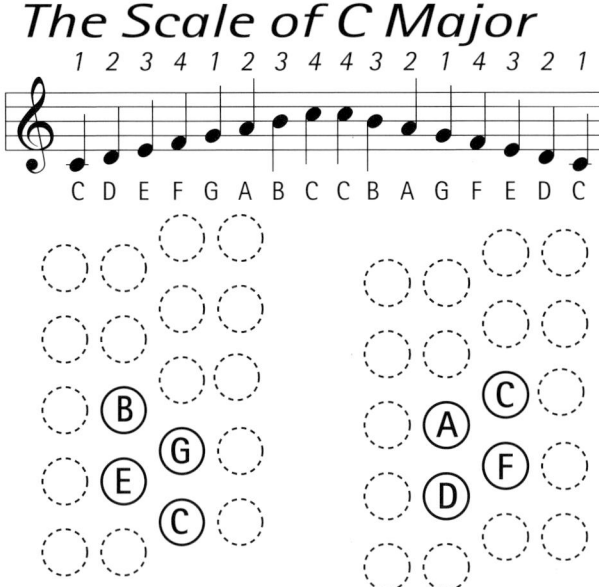

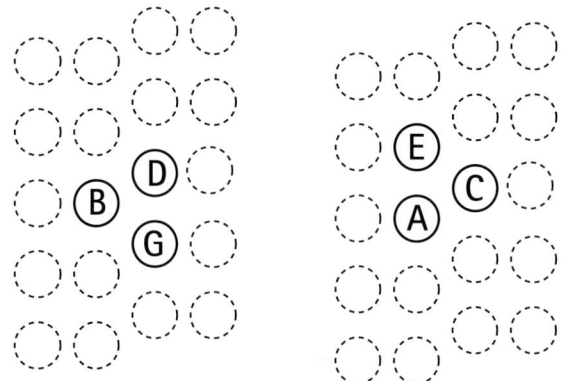

The five lines upon which music is written are known as the "stave". The pitch of a note is indicated by its position on the stave; higher pitched notes are higher up the stave. Any notes too high or too low to fit on the stave are placed on small lines called "leger lines". The English concertina fingering system is cleverly designed so that all the notes in the spaces are played on the right-hand buttons and all those on the lines are played on the left-hand buttons, as can be seen on the fingering chart (page 3).

The scale of C major is the white notes on the piano. On the English concertina, it's the middle two rows. Have a go at playing this scale, it's written out above both musically and diagrammatically. Note names and finger numbers are included in these early tunes and scales. Left-hand fingers are numbered 1, 3 and 5; right-hand fingers are numbered 2, 4 and 6, as shown on the fingering chart (page 3). Play the scale up and down repeatedly until it becomes easy. Notice the regular pattern constantly repeating itself, alternating sides and rows. You can repeat this pattern until you run out of buttons. Try it, it's an excellent exercise. If you're playing a tenor treble, ignore the first button of each row.

Time now to play a tune. We'll start with one you're sure to know, *Little Brown Jug*, an old folk song made famous by none other than Glen Miller. Look at the music and notice that the notes G, A, B, C, D and E are required. Check their position on the note-layout, above right. Pull the bellows (indicated by the V symbol) whilst playing the first six notes. You will notice immediately that some notes naturally last longer than others. Time duration is indicated by using different note symbols. The hollow notes are called "minims"; they last twice as long as the solid notes which are called "crotchets". Now play on to the end of the tune changing bellows direction where indicated. Be careful to keep the air pressure equal in both directions.

Notice that the music is divided up into small, equal sections by vertical lines. These sections are called "bars". The vertical lines are called "bar lines"; thick double bar lines signify the end of a tune and thin double bar lines mark the end of a part or section. Traditional tunes are made up of four bar phrases; in each phrase there is a 'question' and an 'answer'. Although there are no hard and fast rules, it's important, where possible, to change bellows direction between phrases. However, in these early tunes, we'll change every two bars. Experienced players might at times stray away from these fixed points, taking factors such as tempo and dynamics into considerations. Bellows direction changes should be indiscernible to the listener.

Before playing a tune, it's a good idea to open the bellows slightly to ensure you have a large enough reservoir of air. So draw a small amount of air into the bellows and play *Go Tell Aunt Rhody*, a well-known American folk song. Look at the music and notice that the notes C, D, E, F and G are required to play this tune. Check their position on the note-layout, above left. In bar 6 notice more new notes joined together. These are called "quavers". They have a duration of half a crotchet. Single quavers look like this ♪ but are grouped together when they occur in twos and fours. In bar 8 there's a new kind of note, hollow without a stem. It's called a "semibreve". It lasts twice as long as a minim, four times the length of a crotchet.

Go Tell Aunt Rhody

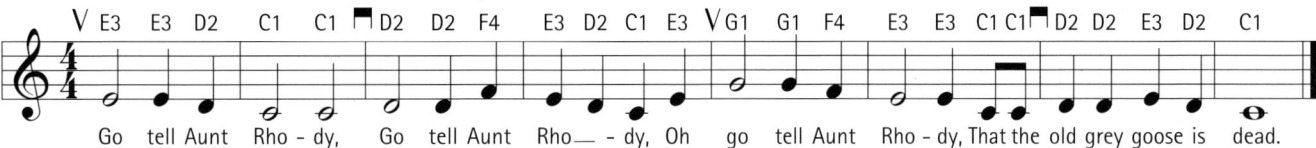

The English Concertina Absolute Beginners

Introducing the Musical Ladder

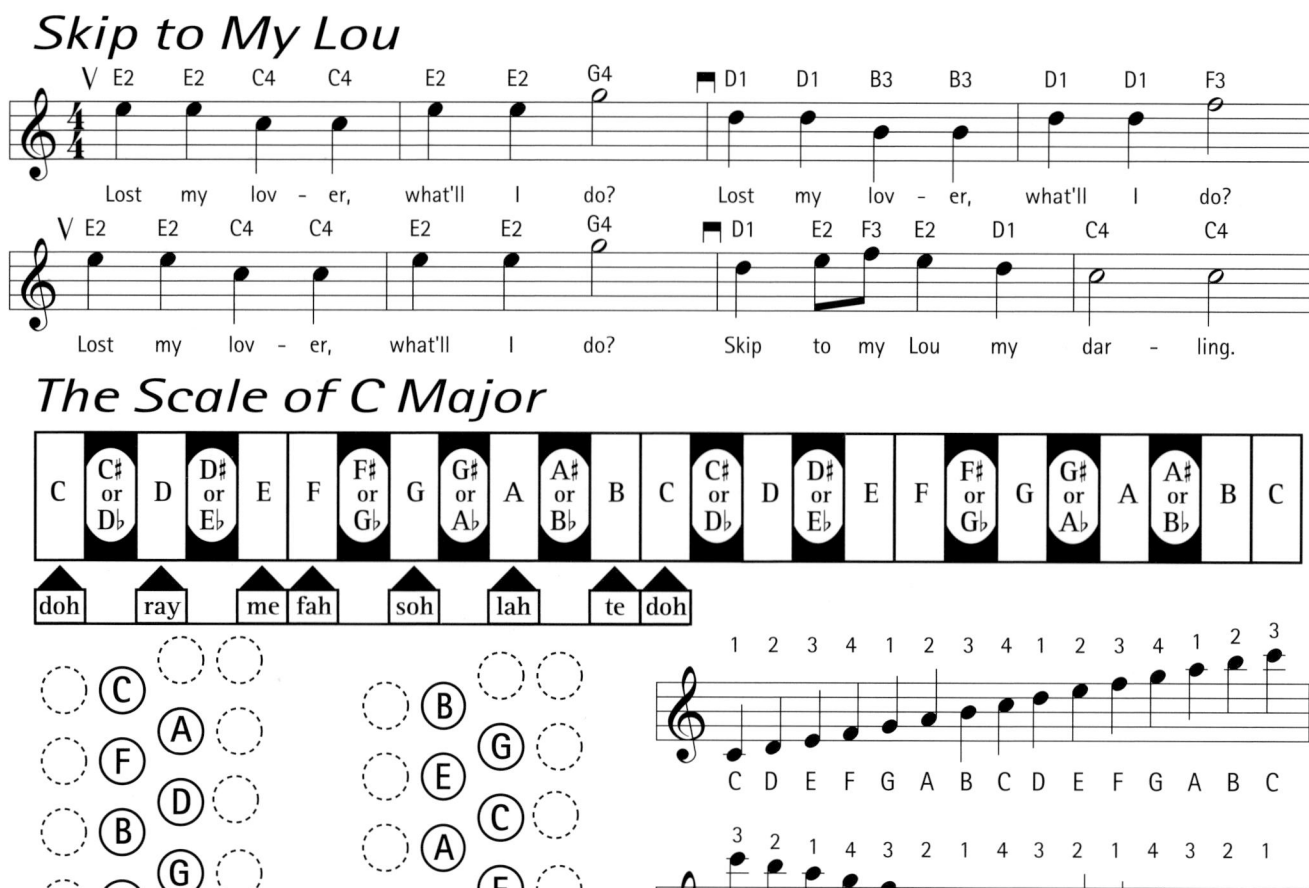

The musical ladder above is derived from the piano keyboard. It shows the notes of music ascending from left to right. Each note is one step of the ladder. The smallest step of the ladder is one "semitone". Two steps of the ladder are one "tone". Musical notes are named after the first seven letters of the alphabet, A to G. These are the white steps of the ladder. The notes shown in the black steps do not have letter names of their own, they take their names from the nearest white ones. For example, the black step between C and D is C plus one semitone or D minus one semitone, C sharp or D flat in musical terminology. After twelve steps (seven white steps) the pattern repeats itself as do the names of the notes. The eighth step (counting the starting step as one) has the same letter name as the first and is said to be one octave higher. A major scale, the familiar doh, ray, me, fah, soh, lah, te, doh, ascends in intervals of tone, tone, semitone, tone, tone, tone, semitone. A scale is named by its first note,

doh. Underneath the ladder is a slider, with this sequence of intervals marked. By moving the slider, you can easily find the notes of any major scale. The slider, in its position above, tells us that the scale of C major is C, D, E, F, G, A, B, C; it contains no sharp or flat notes and it's played on the white notes of the piano.

Practise the scale of C in two octaves, both ascending and descending, as shown in the music and note-layout above. Walk your fingers up each side alternately. Repeat this exercise until you can play it with ease.

A couple of easy tunes to play now. *Skip to My Lou* is a simple tune, great for American western square dances. *Lightly Row*, a children's nursery rhyme, was originally a traditional German folk and children's song called *Hänschen Klein* (*Little Hans*). Finger 1 plays row 2 left, finger 2 plays row 2 right, finger 3 plays row 3 left, and finger 4 plays row 3 right.

Introducing the Key of G Major

Shepherds' Hey

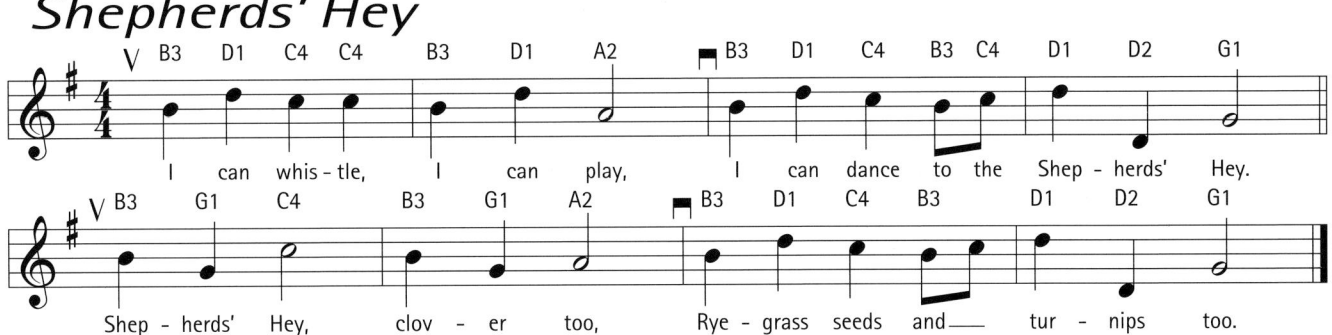

The Scale of G Major

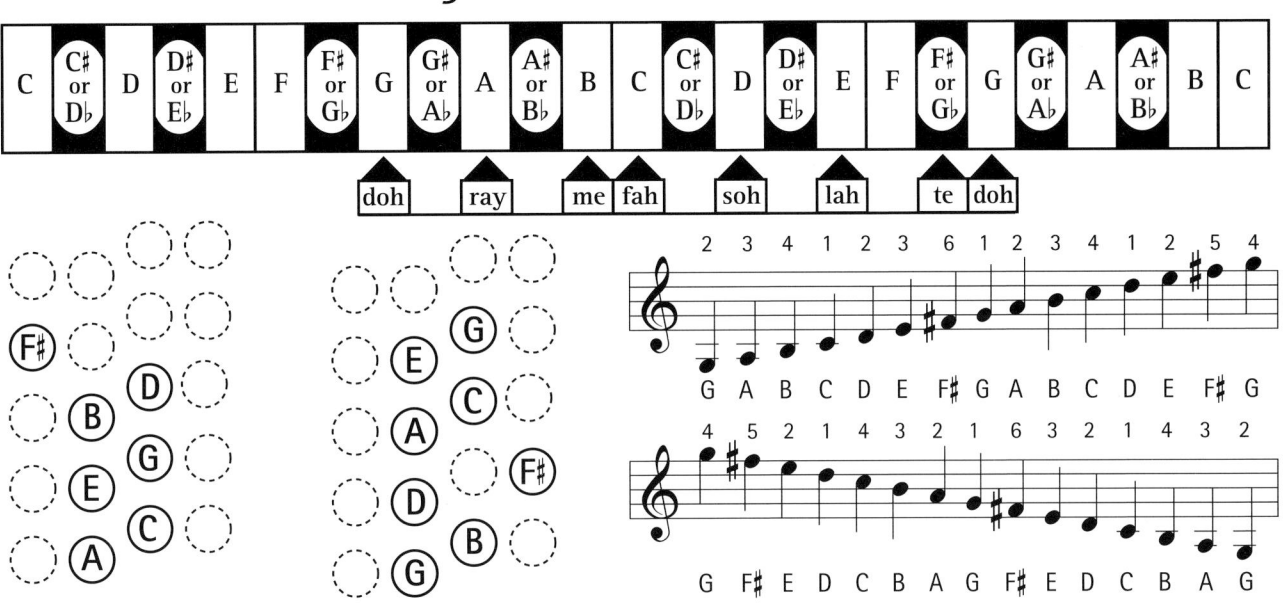

Although C major is a straightforward key, it rarely occurs in traditional music. G major, D major, A major, E minor and A minor are the usual keys. These are the keys we'll be tackling in this book. The 'major' part of the key name is usually assumed and left out, for instance C major is usually just called C.

Now move the slider until doh is adjacent to the note G and read off the scale of G major, G, A, B, C, D, E, F sharp, G. There is one black note, F sharp. A tune using this scale would be said to be in the key of G and all Fs would be sharp. Rather than writing a sharp symbol in front of every F note in the tune, it's found once at the beginning of each line of the music. This is called the "key signature". One sharp in the key signature indicates the tune is in the key of G or its related minor. Practise the scale of G in two octaves, both ascending and descending, as shown in the music and note-layout above. Repeat this exercise until you can play it with ease. Notice, when playing these scales, that all notes one octave apart are on opposite sides of the instrument.

Time to play some more tunes. *Shepherds' Hey* is a very easy Cotswold morris tune from the village of Adderbury in Oxfordshire. F sharp doesn't occur, so although the tune is in G, only the central rows are required. *Bobby Shaftoe* is a Northumbrian tune, used extensively by longsword sides. Watch out for the F sharps, play them on row 4 with finger 6.

Bobby Shaftoe

The English Concertina Absolute Beginners

Introducing 4/4 Time

This Old Man

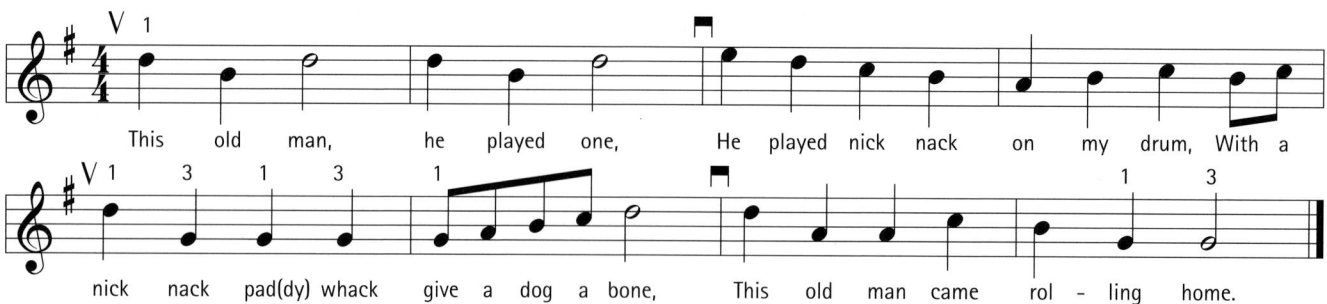

Counting 4/4 Time

Traditional music for the English concertina always has a "treble clef" sign (the curvy symbol) at the beginning of each line of music. Next comes the key signature. On the first line, after the key signature comes the "time signature" which resembles a fraction. The top number denotes the number of counts per bar. The bottom number denotes the type of note that receives one count.

4 = ♩ (crotchet)   8 = ♪ (quaver)

Thus: 2/4 means 2 crotchets to the bar
4/4 means 4 crotchets to the bar
3/4 means 3 crotchets to the bar
6/8 means 6 quavers to the bar
9/8 means 9 quavers to the bar

Let's try counting 4/4 time. Tap your foot at an even pace, say one tap a second, and count **1**, 2, **3**, 4, **1**, 2, **3**, 4 and so on. Put a stress on 1 and a gentler stress on 3, these are the main beats. They are the on-beats, the other two being the off-beats. Each count is one crotchet, minims have two counts. Two quavers share a count; use the word 'and' (say an') to count quavers that don't fall on the beats.

It's time now to bring up one of the most important aspects of playing the English concertina, good fingering technique. Where possible, use a 'new finger' to play the next button. Playing two consecutive buttons with the same finger tends to be undesirable; it's usually far too slow and inefficient and can easily disrupt the flow of a phrase. The basic fingering technique is to use your first fingers to play the top two rows on each side, the second finger for the third row and the third finger for the bottom row. These are always our first choice fingers. This is perfectly straightforward until two consecutive notes on the same row occur. In order to select a 'new finger' we are forced to use a second choice finger, often called cross fingering. Where cross fingering is required, finger numbers have been placed over the notes; use the first choice finger anywhere else. It's important to play the lower note with the higher numbered finger. This is easy when the higher note come first but when the lower note comes first we have to think ahead.

In bar 5 of *This Old Man* we use our second choice finger 3 to play the first G note because we were using finger 1 to play the preceeding D note. We then play 1 3 1 for the following G notes. When a series of more than two repeated notes occurs, it's a good idea to alternate fingers to get the notes sounding clear and crisp. In the last bar we have to think ahead and use our second choice finger to play the last G note so finger 1 is available to play the D note when the tune is repeated. *This Old Man* and *Little Brown Jug* are the classic tunes to play for the ceilidh dance *Pat-a-Cake Polka*. Now play *The Muffin Man*, a good tune for north-west morris. Watch out for the F sharps and the repeated notes. Think ahead in bar 8 and play the G note with finger 3. This music has a new feature, dotted notes. A "dot" after a note means the note's duration is increased by half.

The Muffin Man

Play Some Maritime Melodies

Donkey Riding

New York Girls

OK, that's the baby stuff over; on now to more interesting, but not difficult music. Most of the tunes found in this book are reasonably easy to play. However, the fact that they're easy doesn't mean they are poor or second-rate. They are all excellent and useful tunes just waiting for you to learn and enjoy. They are all currently in use and form a core repertoire for traditional music sessions, ceilidhs, country dances, hoe-downs and morris dancing. It's the player, not the tune, that makes for great music. Here we have four well-known maritime melodies, all excellent tunes for north-west morris.

The sum of notes in a bar of music is always equal to the amount indicated by the time signature. Bars of 3/4 time contain three 'crotchets-worth', bars of 4/4 time contain four 'crotchets-worth' etc. Many tunes start just before the main beat occurs so there is often a short "lead-in" bar at the beginning. This short bar becomes part of the last bar on repeating. The notes missing from the last bar are found in the lead-in bar.

"Pick-up notes" are notes occurring just before the first main beat of a phrase. The lead-in bar contains the pick-up notes of the first phrase of a tune. They can also be found leading into other phrases of a tune. We find them here on this page in *New York Girls* and *Johnny Come Down to Hilo*. It's usually better to change bellows direction on pick-up (terminology for 'before the pick-up notes') rather than on the bar line. Changing bellows direction at these points can make the tune flow more smoothly. Now you've got the feel of your instrument, it's time to play whole phrases on each direction of the bellows.

In traditional music circles, it's usual to play tunes through at least two or three times. So when playing *New York Girls*, *South Australia* and *Johnny Come Down to Hilo*, think ahead and play the final G note of each tune with finger 3, leaving finger 1 available to play the first D note next time through. Think ahead in bar 12 of *Donkey Riding* and change to finger 4 to play the second A note, freeing up finger 2 to play the next E note. You will also need to use second choice fingers in bars 8 and 16 of *Donkey Riding* and bar 14 of *South Australia*.

South Australia

Johnny Come Down to Hilo

The English Concertina Absolute Beginners

9

Introducing Traditional Music

Winster Gallop

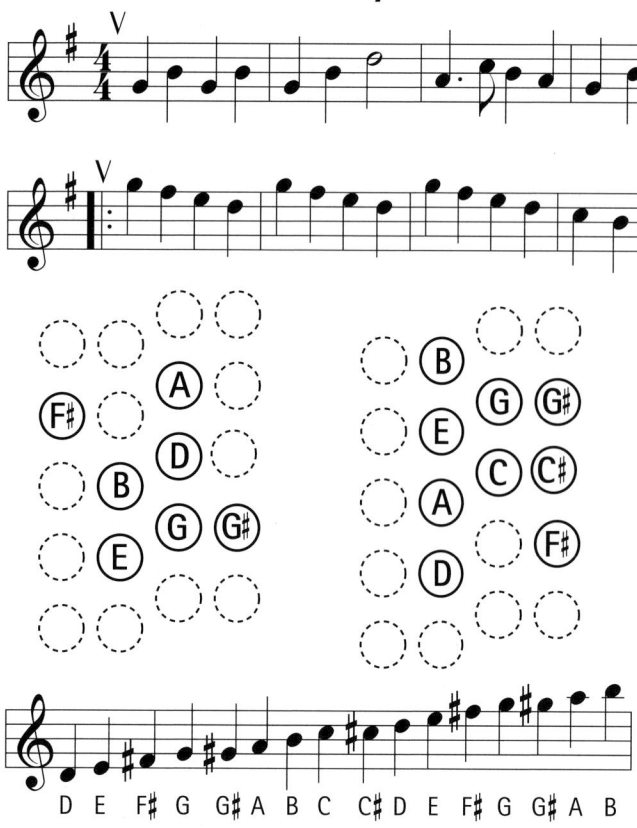

Besides being a tutor for the English concertina, this book is also a collection of traditional tunes from England, Scotland, Wales, Ireland and America. 'Folk' and 'traditional' mean the same thing, but for the sake of clarity, this book is about traditional music as opposed to folk song. Even though some of the tunes do have words, we are only interested in the melody. Every basic rhythm is to be found here: jigs, reels, waltzes, hornpipes, polkas etc. They range from very easy to fairly difficult. However, the majority of tunes are well within the grasp of everyone, but not without practice. Practice is the key to success. You must practise every day, preferably for at least one hour.

The bulk of traditional music and, except for the last two pages, all the tunes in this book are played using only the sixteen notes shown in the music and fingering chart on the left. It's important to know where these notes are to be found on your instrument. With the addition of half a dozen notes occurring less frequently, you have all you need to play traditional music.

The double bar lines with dots facing left mean repeat from the double bar line with dots facing right. If that symbol doesn't occur, repeat from the beginning.

All traditional tunes have at least two parts. Two is the standard but some have three or more. Each part is usually eight bars in length but a few are only four bars in length. Generally each part is repeated before the next is played but occasionally parts are played only once. The first part is called the A music, the second part the B music, third the C music and so on. A typical traditional tune would be played 2 As and 2 Bs.

Only first choice fingers are required to play all three tunes on this page. *Winster Gallop* is the favourite tune of novice players. It's one of the most played tunes at festival sessions and it has its own dance. *Jimmy Allen*, a Scottish tune often called *Jamie Allen*, is very popular with English country dance bands. *Rattlin' Bog* is a rousing tune and a well-known song. You can use it for both Irish set dancing and English country dancing. You will hear it played in music sessions regularly.

Jimmy Allen

Rattlin' Bog

10

The English Concertina Absolute Beginners

Play Some English Tunes

British Grenadiers is a tune used by just about every north-west morris side in England. In bars 3, 5 and 15 we have the series of notes D G B. We can't play the B note with finger 3 as we would have liked because we used it as our second choice finger to play the G note. This means we have to use finger 5, another second choice finger. Difficult at first but practice (as usual) will make this awkward fingering easy.

Uncle Bernard's Polka is a big favourite in English music sessions. Although it isn't necessary to use finger 3, our second choice finger, to play the final G note when repeating the A music, it's a better plan to do so. Sticking to the same fingering throughout a tune lets your 'muscle memory' play the correct note, without you having to think about it. Where you see the brackets play the notes under 1 first time through, then play the notes under 2 on the repeat.

Winster Processional is a morris tune from Derbyshire. It's a version of *The Helston Furry Dance*. *Buttered Peas* is easy to play and is an ideal country dance tune.

The Tip Top Polka is the tune used by the Britannia Coco-nut Dancers of Bacup for their processional dance on Easter Saturday. Notice that the alternating fingers technique features very prominently in the first part of this tune. The curved line joining notes together is called a "tie". A tie joins notes of the same pitch, indicating a single sustained note with a time value of the two (or more) combined.

The English Concertina Absolute Beginners

11

Introducing the Key of D Major

Banbury Bill

The Scale of D Major

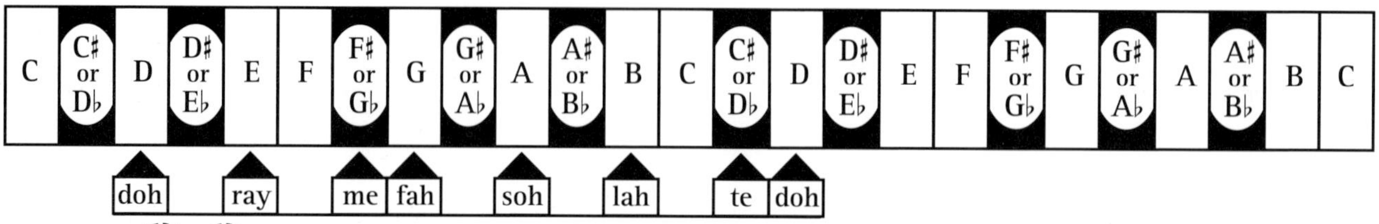

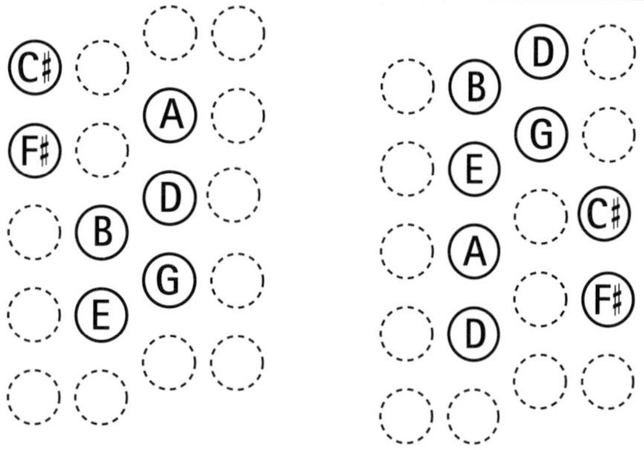

Now move the slider until doh is adjacent to the note D and read off the scale of D major, D, E, F sharp, G, A, B, C sharp, D. We now have two sharps in the key signature, indicating the tune is in the key of D or its related minor. Practise this scale in two octaves, both ascending and descending, as shown in the music and note-layout above. Repeat this exercise until you can play it with ease. Play the low F sharps and low C sharps with finger 6 and the high ones with finger 5.

Banbury Bill is a Cotswold morris tune from the village of Bampton in Oxfordshire. Play the B and E notes here with fingers 3 and 5. They are descending, so choose finger 5 as the second choice finger rather than finger 1.

Harper's Frolic is from Derbyshire and was brought to prominence by the New Victory Band. Think ahead in bar 12 and play the A note with finger 4.

Nelly Bly, a Stephen Foster song, is an ideal country dance tune. Play descending B and E notes with fingers 3 and 5.

Harper's Frolic

Nelly Bly

Play Some Country Dance Tunes

My Love She's but a Lassie Yet

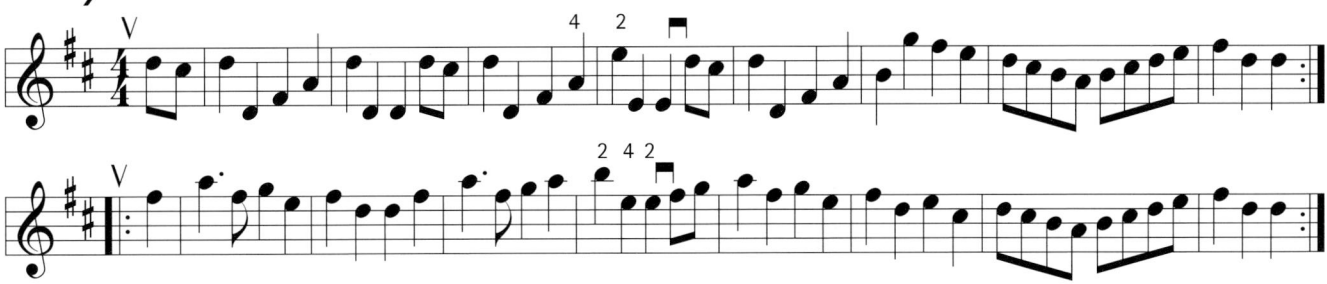

I Have a Bonnet Trimmed with Blue

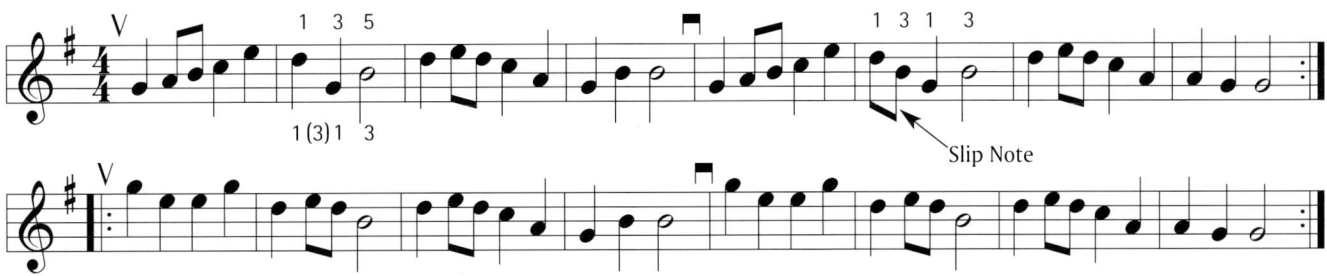

Slip Note

All the above instruments are known as concertinas. However, strictly speaking, only six sided models are concertinas; eight sided models are called aeolas and twelve sided models are called edeophones.

My Love She's but a Lassie Yet is a Scottish tune, often used for the ceilidh dance *Cumberland Square Eight*. Think ahead in bar 3 and play the A note with second choice finger 4.

I Have a Bonnet Trimmed with Blue is often played as a fast Irish polka. Note the D G B sequence again, play it 1 3 5. Alternatively you can simplify the fingering by slipping in an extra B note (we'll call it a 'slip note') as shown in bar 6. Now the fingering 1 3 1 3 is easy.

The Huntsman's Chorus was originally a chorus in the 1821 opera *Der Freischütz* by Carl Maria von Weber. It found its way into the repertoire of country fiddlers and soon the version we know today evolved. It became particularly popular in Yorkshire where it has its own dance. Use the alternating fingers technique in bar 9.

The Rose Tree is in the repertoire of most country dance bands. It's found in Ireland under the name *Portláirge*.

You will hear all these tunes played at ceilidhs, music sessions and folk festivals.

The Huntsman's Chorus

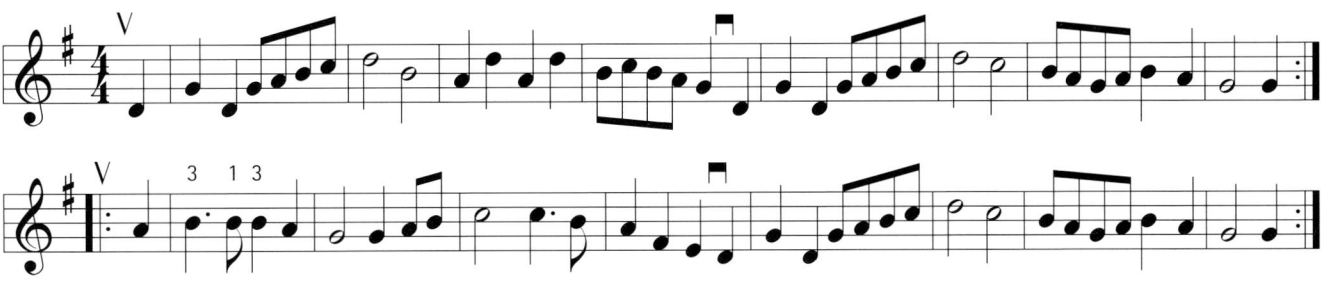

The Rose Tree

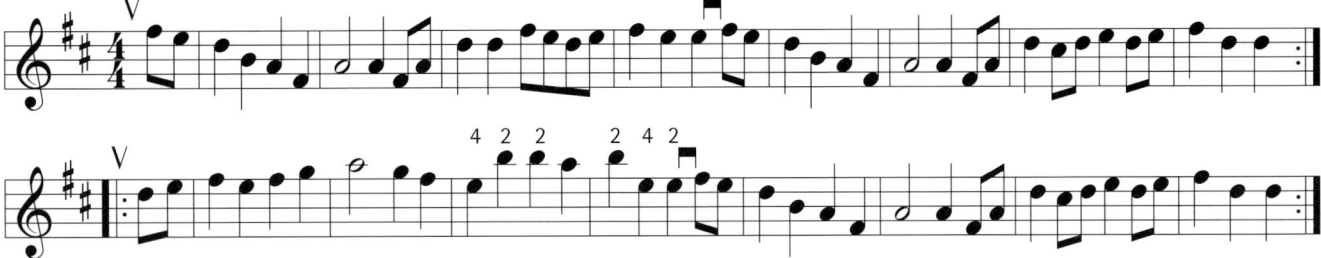

The English Concertina   Absolute Beginners

Introducing 6/8 Time

Cock of the North

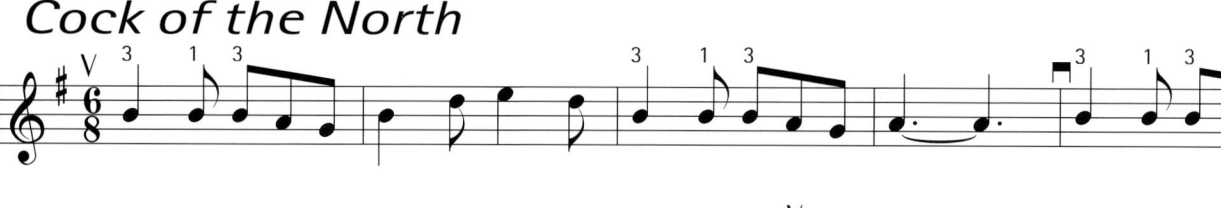

Counting 6/8 Time

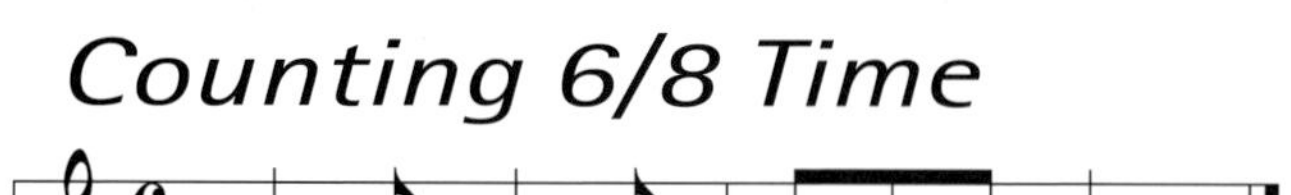

Humpty sat on a Humpty Dumpty, Humpty sat on a wa_all,
Humpty sat on a Humpty Dumpty, Humpty sat on a wa_all.
Humpty Dumpty, Humpty Dumpty, Humpty sat on a wa_all,
Humpty Dumpty, Humpty Dumpty, Humpty sat on a wa_all.

Now let's have a look at 6/8 time, six quavers to the bar, the time signature of jigs. Single jigs are characterized by a predominance of crotchet/quaver pairs, whereas double jigs have predominance of groups of three quavers. Although there are six quavers to the bar, there are only two main beats; count **1 an' 2 an' 1 an' 2 an'**, in the rhythm of the words Humpty Dumpty Humpty Dumpty.

Cock of the North is a single jig and probably the best known Scottish tune. You can play it for the *Gay Gordons* - you're sure to know it. In Ireland, it's usually known as *Chase Me Charlie*. Notice the use of the alternating fingers technique to play the recurring B notes. Try using *Humpty Dumpty* to get the rhythm. When you see the notes ♩♪ sing *Humpty*, when you see the notes ♩♪♩♪ sing *Humpty Dumpty*, when you see the notes ♫ sing *sat on a*, and when you see the notes ♩. sing a long *wall*, that is, hold it for twice as long as in the nursery rhyme. Give it a try, it's a good laugh.

MacNamara's Band is an old Irish parlour song made famous by Bing Crosby in the 1940s. This tune makes an excellent military two-step, a subtle variation of the single jig. Repeated notes are a major feature in this tune and here our alternating fingers trick is a godsend. Listen to the soundtrack and notice alternate long and short notes, a typical feature of single jigs. Because the final note is long, rather than cross fingering, simply steal a 'quavers-worth of time' to move finger 1 from the G button to the D button when the tune is repeated. This tune has many extremely long notes; take great care to give them their full length.

Where the sharp symbol occurs in front of the C notes play C sharp instead of C natural. This is called an "accidental", a note foreign to the scale indicated by the key signature. An accidental affects all notes after it on that line or space within the bar in which it is written. The accidental does not affect notes an octave higher or lower and does not affect notes in subsequent bars.

MacNamara's Band

Play Some Cotswold Morris Tunes

Hey Away

Shave the Donkey

On this page are four well-known Cotswold morris tunes. Each Cotswold tune has its own associated dance.

Hey Away is from the village of Bledington in Gloucestershire. Use your second choice finger 3 to play the final G in the first part so finger 1 is free to play the D on the repeat.

Shave the Donkey has four-bar parts and is an easy tune. It's from the village of Bampton. When repeating the A part, it isn't convenient to play the last G note in bar 4 with finger 3 as in *Hey Away* because we used it to play the preceeding B note. However, because it's a minim, it's easy to steal a 'quavers-worth of time' and use finger 1 for both the G note and the first D note.

Laudanum Bunches is from the village of Headington in Oxfordshire. *Swaggering Boney* is from the village of Longborough in Gloucestershire. It makes sense to play the cascading sequences at the beginning of the B music all with the same fingering.

Laudanum Bunches

Swaggering Boney

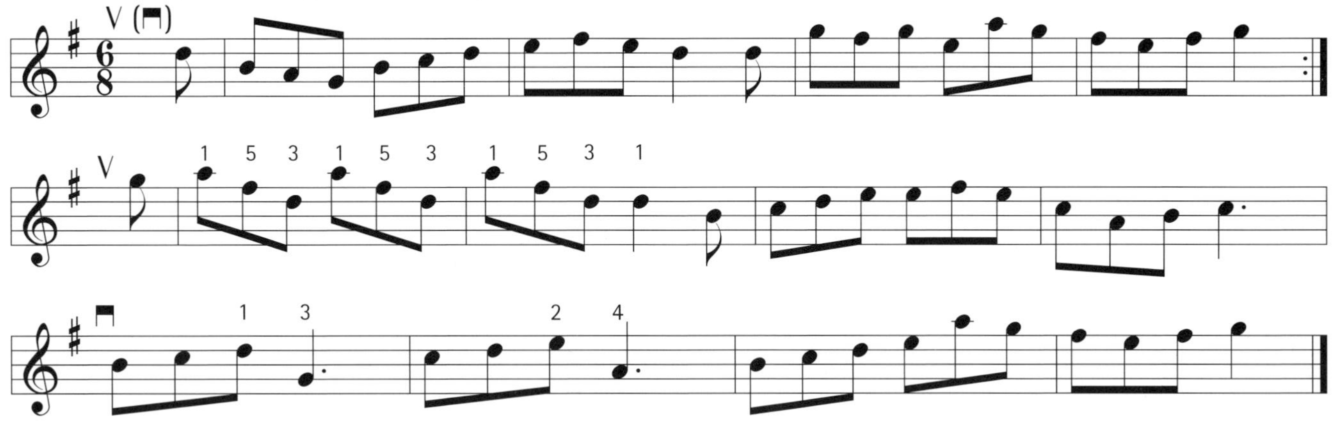

The English Concertina Absolute Beginners

Introducing 3/4 Time

Michael Turner's Waltz

Counting 3/4 Time

1　2　3　　1 (2) 3　　1 2 an' 3 an'　　1 (2) an' 3　　1 an' 2 3

Let's try counting 3/4 time. Tap your left foot once then your right foot twice at an even pace and count **1**, **2**, **3**, **1**, **2**, **3** and so on. Each count is one crotchet. Minims have two counts. Two quavers share a count; use the word 'and' (say an') to count quavers that don't fall on the beats.

Michael Turner's Waltz is from Sussex. It's a big favourite at English pub sessions. Michael Turner was a 19th Century fiddler and shoemaker from Warnham in Sussex. Although the tune now bears his name, it was originally composed by Mozart.

The South Wind is an Irish old-time waltz, much faster than the modern waltz. When going to the B music we have a choice of fingering options. We can be consistant and let 'muscle memory' (call it 'habit' if you like) play the last G with finger 3, then play the lead-in bar with fingers 5 3. Alternatively 'break the habit' and play the last G with finger 1 and use the easier 3 1 fingering for the lead-in bar. You will be often confronted with choices such as this. It's up to the individual as to which choice to make. There are no hard and fast rules on cross fingering but it's a good idea to be as consistent as possible.

Shoe the Donkey is another Irish tune. It has its own dance. It's a varsoviana (also known as a varsovienne). This type of tune originated in Warsaw, Poland.

The South Wind

Shoe the Donkey

Play Some Welsh Tunes

Sweet Jenny Jones

All Through the Night

Sweet Jenny Jones is a lovely waltz from Wales. It's used for a dance by Adderbury morris dancers. It has an eight-bar A music played twice and a sixteen-bar B music played once.

All Through the Night is a beautiful Welsh folk song. Its name in Welsh is *Ar Hyd y Nos*. The tune has been around for centuries and featured in *The Beggar's Opera*.

Men of Harlech occupies an important place in Welsh national culture. The song gained international recognition when it was featured prominently in the 1964 film Zulu. This tune is widely used as a regimental march. There are numerous versions of the song; however the tune doesn't change and that is what we are interested in.

In these tunes we find some new musical symbols. They are called "rests". A rest in music is a period of silence; the length of which is specified by the shape, and sometimes also the position of the symbol. The symbol 𝄽 indicates a period of silence which has the length of one crotchet. The symbol ▬, when it sits on the middle line, indicates a period of silence which has the length of one minim. When this symbol hangs from the fourth line (from the bottom), it indicates a period of silence which has the length of one semibreve.

Men of Harlech

The English Concertina Absolute Beginners

Introducing 2/4 Time

Camptown Races

Counting 2/4 Time

1   2   1 an' 2 er an' er   1 (2) an 1 an' er 2 (an') er 1 (2)

To the player of traditional music, 2/4 time is basically 4/4 but faster. Unlike classical music traditional tunes are not written on tablets of stone; they can be interpreted in a variety of ways. 2/4, 2/2 and 4/4 time are, as often as not, interchangeable. Traditional tunes can undergo substantial changes. Many reels, when slowed down, turn naturally into hornpipes. Jigs, when slowed down, can easily be turned into waltzes and so on. Other changes can be more subtle; for instance, notes can be added, deleted, lengthened or shortened for variation, to help with fingering or for simplification to make a tune playable. The new notes introduced here are called "semiquavers". They have the duration of half a quaver. On their own they look like this ♪.

Camptown Races is a well-known American tune written by Stephen Foster. It was originally called *Gwine to Run All Night*. It's a great tune for the western squares. It's good to finish each part on finger 3, leaving finger 1 free to start the 1 3 1 fingering at the beginning of each part. In the A music this fingering is used to cope with the repeated notes. In the B music, it's used to deal with consecutive notes on the same row. *Egan's Polka* takes its name from a player of the tune. It's sometimes called *The Kerry Polka*. It's a brilliant tune and one of the simplest of all. It's found at the beginning of many Irish music instructional books. *Chinese Breakdown* is fabulous, it has its own dance with a singing call. It's one of the best loved dances at ceilidhs. Notice there is an accidental in bar 27, indicated by the natural symbol ♮. Instead of playing C sharp, play C natural.

Egan's Polka

Chinese Breakdown

Play Some American Reels

Buffalo Girls

The Road to Boston

American reels (single reels that is) are written in 2/4 time. They are played at quite a fast pace. The tunes on this page are all typical of this genre, and although they were all originally songs, the melodies are ideal for western squares.

In bar 3 of *Buffalo Girls*, it isn't convenient to play the A note with finger 4 because we used it to play the preceding C note; also the theoretical 6 4 2 fingering is a tad awkward. Simplify the fingering by adding a 'slip note'. Change the A crotchet to A dotted quaver and C semiquaver, then the fingering 4 2 4 2 is easy. Or simply 'steal' time from the A crotchet and play 4 2 2. Altering the melody slightly is often an excellent solution to deal with awkward fingering and is perfectly acceptable in traditional music.

When playing *The Road to Boston* and *Uncle Reuben*, be sure to use the alternating fingers technique where indicated. *Angelina Baker* is another Stephen Foster tune and is absolutely brilliant. Stephen Foster, originally from Pennsylvania, was a composer of parlour and minstrel songs in the era leading up to the American Civil War.

Uncle Reuben

Angelina Baker

The English Concertina Absolute Beginners

Introducing Slip Jigs and Slides

Slip jigs are found mainly in Ireland and Northumberland. They are in 9/8 time, nine quavers to the bar. Each bar is half as long again as an ordinary jig so there are three main beats to the bar. Looking at it another way, each bar goes to the rhythm Humpty Dumpty Humpty.

Slides are fast dance tunes from Sliabh Luachra, an area straddling the border of Kerry and Cork in the south-west of Ireland. Slides are simply fast single jigs. They are written in 12/8 time, twelve quavers in each bar. The bars are twice as long as those in jigs but there are only half as many. Two bars of a slide are a whole phrase. When playing slip jigs and slides you might find it preferable to open and close bellows every two bars. These time signatures sound quite daunting but you'll soon find out they're pretty straightforward. Only first choice fingers are required to play all four tunes on this page, allowing you to concentrate solely on these new time signatures.

Drops of Brandy is probably the best known slip jig of all, cropping up all over Britain and Ireland. The tune is often played in the key of A. *Drops of Brandy* has its own dance featuring that most popular ceilidh dance figure *Strip the Willow*. Notice on the soundtrack the extra G note so that the tune resolves to the key note to finish.

When slides are used for Irish set dancing they are played at a tremendously fast speed (on the soundtrack the pace is kept nice and steady) so you might like to try changing fingers when playing repeated notes, as shown in *The Star Above the Garter*. Many slides and polkas don't have proper names so they are often called by the names of musicians who play them a lot. *Dennis Enright's Slide* is one such tune.

Scotland is from the tenth edition of *Playford's English Dancing Master*, published in 1698. It crops up all over Britain and Ireland under various names. It's particularly popular in Northumberland under the name of *Andrew Carr*.

Play Some Sliabh Luachra Tunes

The Brosna Slide is also known as *The Lonesome Road to Dingle* and *Trip to the Jacks*.

Maggie in the Wood is probably the best known Irish polka. Notice the new symbol at the end of each part, it's a rest which has the duration of one quaver.

Scattery Island is quite easy and sounds brilliant. It's named after an uninhabited island in the River Shannon estuary; situated off the coast of Clare, one mile from Kilrush. Good players of traditional music like to play variations on each successive repeat. Play the variations shown here; use the ascending notes to lead into the A music and the descending notes to lead into the B music.

Tom Sullivan's Polka has a long B music. Notice how the melody returns to the A music in the last three bars. This characteristic is often found in this type of tune. Be sure to play the C natural accidentals where indicated. Notice in bars 10 and 18, the change of finger to play the two A notes; an excellent standard fingering manoeuvre, similar to that suggested in *The Star Above the Garter*. This same technique is also used to play the D notes in bars 8 and 16.

Besides being famous for its slides, Sliabh Luachra (pronounced Sleeve Loocra, meaning The Rushy Mountain) is even better known for its polkas, often called Kerry polkas. Polkas and slides are played at a mighty pace for the set dances of the area, dances such as *The North Kerry Set*, *The Ballybunion Set* and *The Kenmare Polka Set*.

The English Concertina Absolute Beginners

21

Introducing the Key of E Minor

God Rest Ye Merry Gentlemen

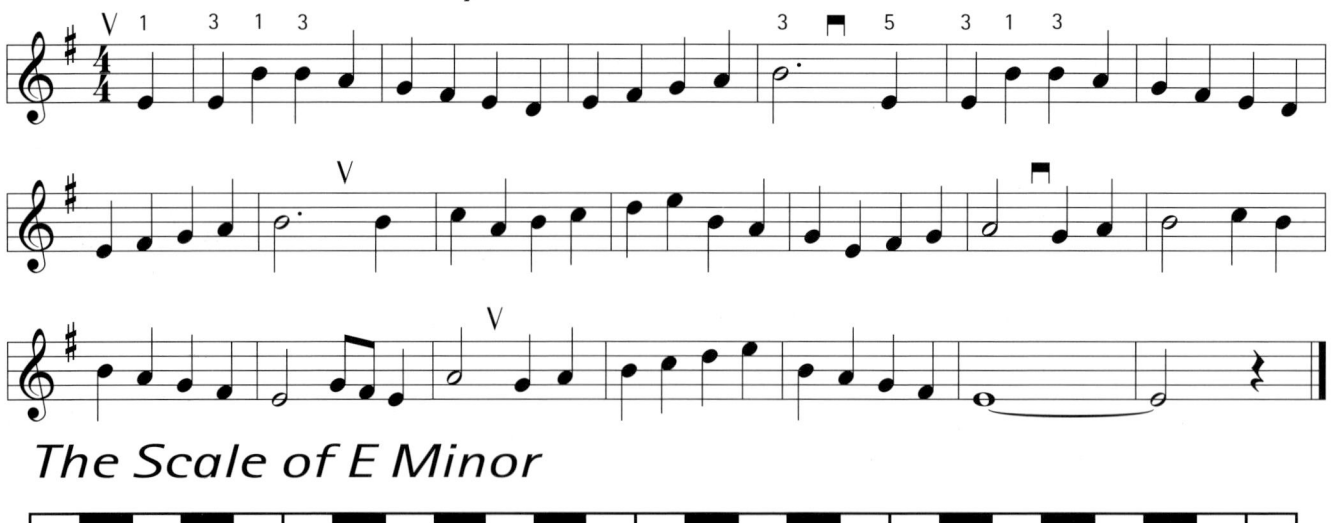

The Scale of E Minor

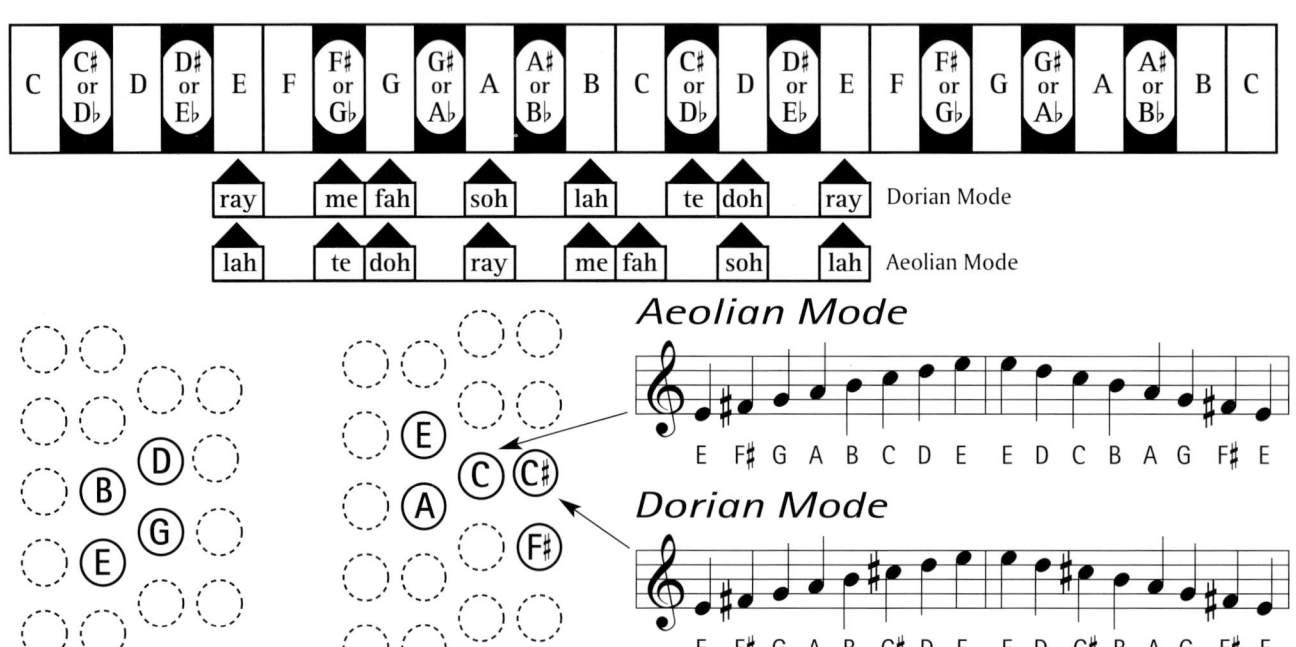

Minor keys in traditional music occur in what are known as modes. They can be either aeolian (lah mode) which follows the white notes of the piano keyboard starting at A, or dorian (ray mode) which follows the white notes starting at D. Dorian mode is the most common in traditional music. If we position the sliders so that ray (dorian mode) and lah (aeolian mod) are adjacent to E we can read off their respective scales. The key of E minor aeolian mode has one sharp in the key signature, and E minor dorian mode has two. Practise the E minor scales shown here, both ascending and descending, until you can play them with ease.

God Rest Ye Merry Gentlemen is a Christmas carol everybody knows. It makes a really good reel and is a great tune to play in sessions over the Christmas period. Notice the fingering. In bars 1 and 5, the notes E and B are ascending so finger 1 is our second choice finger. In bar 4, the notes B and E are descending so finger 5 is our second choice finger.

The Rigged Ship is in the key of E minor dorian mode. It's a variant of a Scottish tune called the *Hills of Glenorchy*. At first glance you would expect to play the first two notes, B E, with fingers 3 and 5. However, on the repeats we are playing E B E, therefore it's fingers 3 1 3. Keep the same fingering in bar 5 to avoid confusing 'muscle memory'. An alternative fingering is shown under the stave which you might prefer.

The Rigged Ship

Play Some Playford Tunes

Playford tunes are tunes published by John Playford and his son, Henry, in the seventeenth century. John Playford, born in 1623, became a London bookseller and publisher. He was not the composer of the tunes, although it's possible that he might have made some small contribution. His best known publication was *The English Dancing Master*, published in 1651. The book contained both the music and dance instructions for 105 English country dances. These dances were aimed at the educated classes. Subsequent editions were published, and over the next century or so, many new tunes and dances were added. These are the tunes we know as Playford tunes and they have quite a distinct style.

Newcastle is probably the best known Playford tune of all. This tune, along with *Grimstock*, were published in the first edition.

The word 'maggot' is found in several Playford tune titles, it can mean a tune that goes round and round in your brain and you can't shift it. It can be best translated as 'favourite' or 'fancy'. It's akin to words in Irish tune titles like 'humours' and 'planxty'.

Playford dances all have their own individual tunes, and usually the dance and the tune have the same name. However, *Hunt the Squirrel* is the tune which is played for the dance *The Geud Man of Ballangigh*.

The English Concertina   Absolute Beginners

Introducing the Key of A Minor

Tralee Gaol

The Scale of A Minor

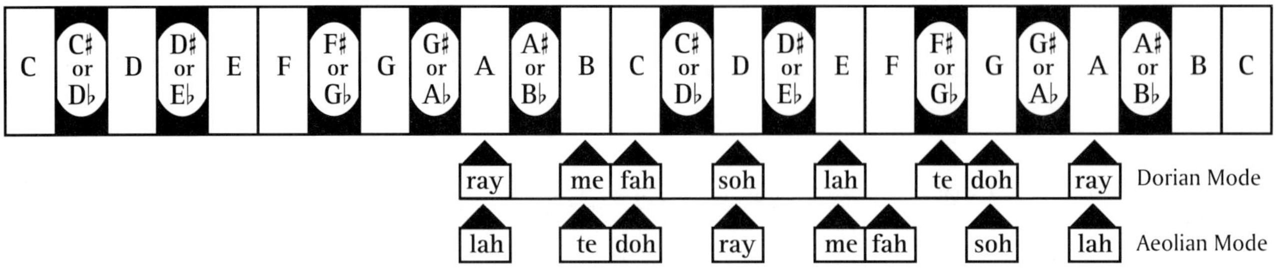

Aeolian Mode

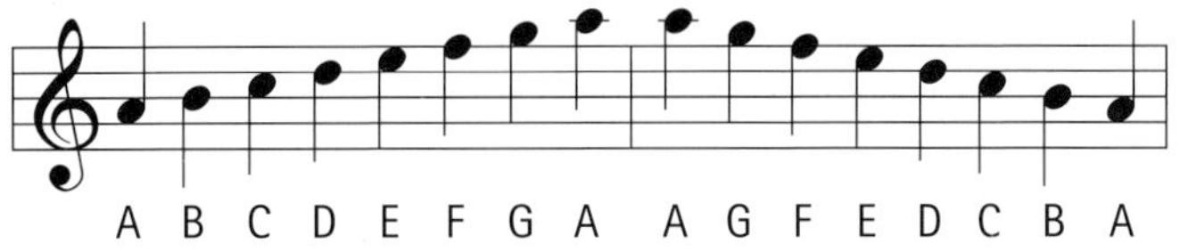

Dorian Mode

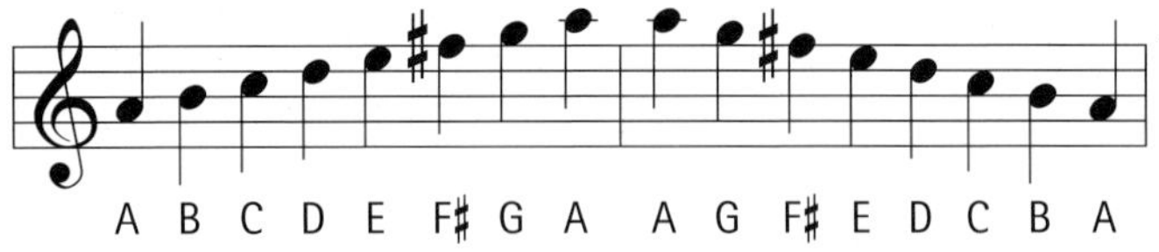

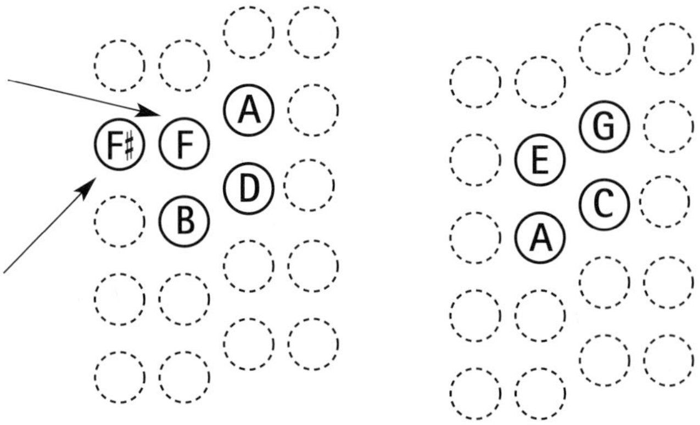

If we position the sliders so that ray (dorian mode) and lah (aeolian mod) are adjacent to A we can read off their respective scales. The key of A minor aeolian mode has no sharps in the key signature, and A minor dorian mode has one. Practise these scales until you can play them with ease.

Tralee Gaol is a variant of the Scottish song *The Haughs o' Cromdale*. Tralee is a town in West Kerry, Ireland. This tune is in A minor aeolian mode. However, this is a little ambiguous as it contains neither F natural nor F sharp. Change from first choice finger 2 to second choice finger 4 at the end of each part, ready to play the next E note.

Spancil Hill is in A minor dorian mode. It's a beautiful Irish waltz. It's also a song about someone who has emigrated to California, dreaming about being back home in the small village of Spancil Hill in County Clare.

Spancil Hill

Play Some Irish Tunes

The Enniskillen Dragoon

Sonny's Mazurka

The Enniskillen Dragoon is a march. Enniskillen is a town on the shores of Lough Erne in County Fermanagh, Ulster.

Sonny's Mazurka is the best known Irish mazurka. Mazurkas originate from Poland. They were brought to Ireland by military regiments. This type of tune is played mainly in Donegal in the very north-west of Ireland.

Rakes of Mallow is a single reel sometimes known as *The Polka*. It's extremely well-known throughout Britain and Ireland and is hugely popular with ceilidh bands and morris sides.

The Derry Boat is a single jig. It takes its name from the ferry, commonly known as the Cattle Boat, on which Donegal emigrants and travellers sailed back and forth from Derry to Glasgow. Passengers were crammed aboard; just like the cattle, whose strong smell permeated every corner of the ship. The ferry was still in operation right up to the 1960s. Note the extensive use of alternating fingers.

Rakes of Mallow

The Derry Boat

The English Concertina Absolute Beginners

Introducing the Hornpipe Rhythm

The Keel Row

Katie Bairdie

Hornpipes are similar to slow double reels but with a much more pronounced beat and bouncy rhythm. This is due to the long/short note groupings, often referred to as a dotted rhythm. Reels and hornpipes can be interchangeable. Slow a reel down, bounce it up and it becomes a hornpipe, and vice versa. For this reason music for hornpipes is written in 4/4 time. Unfortunately the mathematics doesn't quite work out. The way they are written indicates that the long note is thrice the duration of the short one. However, to play this genre correctly, the long note has to be only twice as long as the short one. To be musically correct, hornpipes really should be written in 12/8 time. This is not a problem as players of traditional music are familiar with this dotted 4/4 time concept (whether they know it or not) and adjust accordingly. In this type of tune it can be preferable to open and close bellows every two bars.

The Keel Row is a Northumbrian hornpipe which very easily converts to a reel, jig or march. *Katie Bairdie* is a Scottish tune and is often called *Kafoozalum*. It's the nursery rhyme *London Bridge is Falling Down*. Play the final G note of both parts with finger 3 when going to the A music and finger 1 when going to the B music. *Some Say the Devil's Dead*, sometimes called *Love Will You Marry Me*, is the Irish version of a Scottish tune called *The Braes o' Mar*.

In this type of tune, where semiquaver/dotted-quaver pairs of the same note occur, it's well worth going to the trouble of changing finger to play the second note of the pair, even if it means having to use a second choice finger to play the preceding or following note.

In Ireland all these tunes would be classed as barn dances, flings, highlands or Germans. As far as we are concerned, at this moment they are all hornpipes.

Green Grow the Rushes

Some Say the Devil's Dead

Play Some Northumbrian Tunes

Salmon Tails up the Water

Hexham Races

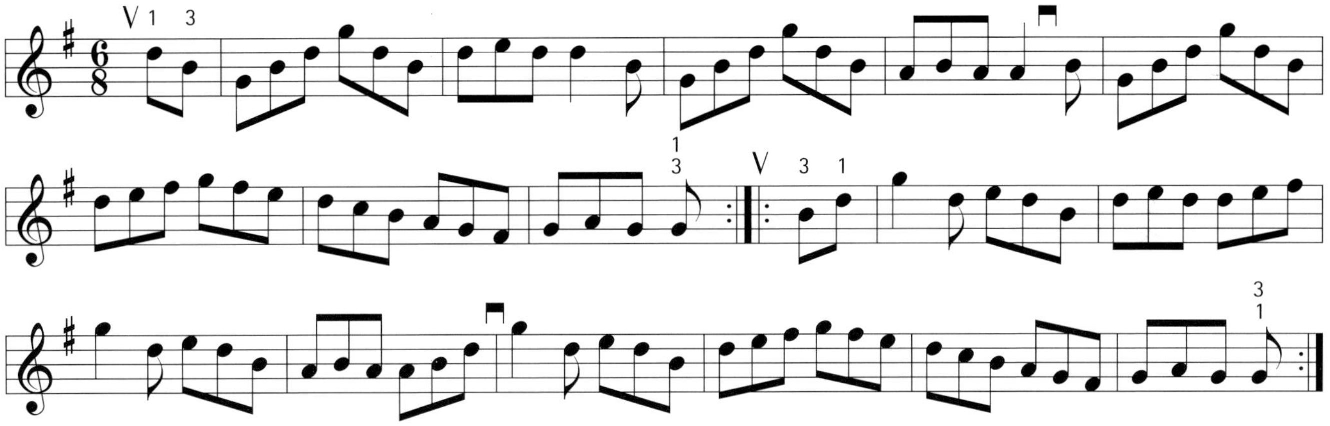

Salmon Tails Up the Water is a great favourite at festival sessions and is massively popular with north-west morris sides.

Hexham Races is a jig well-known in Northumberland. It can be found in O'Neill's Dance Music of Ireland as *I Will if I Can*. There is a Scottish variant called *Kenmure's on an' Awa' Willie*. When going to the A music, use the fingering 3 1 3, when going to the B music, use the fingering 1 3 1.

The Redesdale Hornpipe contains a new feature, triplets, three notes with a bracket and a 3. This means that the three notes are played in the space of two. This tune was composed by James Hill and named *Underhand*, after a famous racehorse. The original key was B flat. In recent times the parts have been reversed, the key has been transposed, the tune has been altered to fit the range of the Northumbrian smallpipes and the name has been changed. Redesdale is a valley of spectacular natural beauty lying in the heart of Northumberland.

The Redesdale Hornpipe

The English Concertina Absolute Beginners

Introducing the Key of A Major

A Hundred Pipers

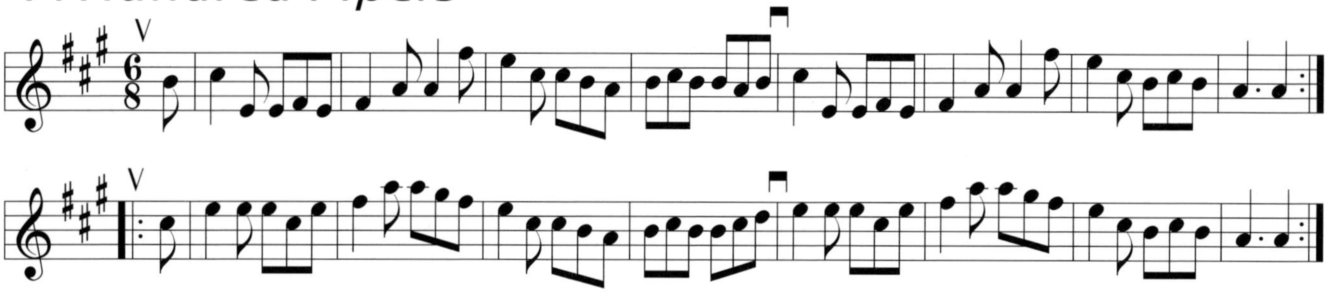

The Scale of A Major

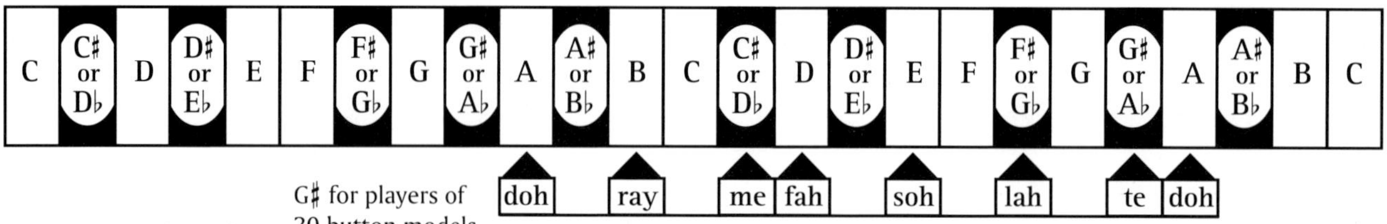

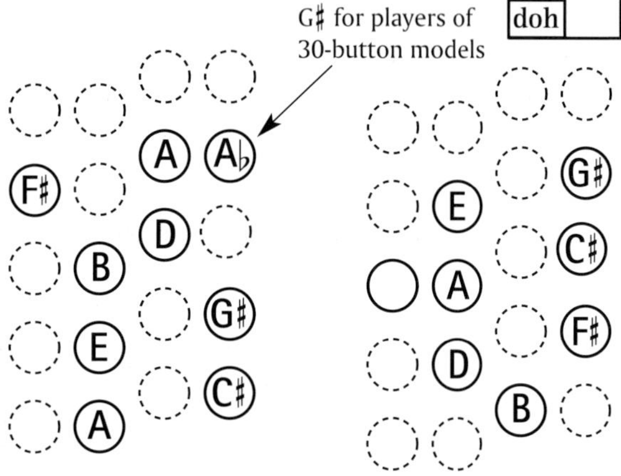

Now move the major key slider until doh is adjacent to the note A and read off the scale of A major, A, B, C sharp, D, E, F sharp, G sharp, A. We now have three sharps in the key signature, indicating the tune is in the key of A or its related minor. Practise this scale in two octaves, both ascending and descending, as shown in the music and note-layout above. Repeat this exercise until you can play it with ease. Players of 30-button instruments will have to use the left-hand G sharp (A flat) button as the right-hand G sharp button is missing from these concertinas. Unfortunately, this left-hand position is not as convenient as the right-hand one found on larger models.

A Hundred Pipers is a Scottish single jig. It's also the tune for a well-known song. *Roxburgh Castle* is a Scottish hornpipe often used for a Cotswold morris solo jig from Bampton called *Fool's Jig*. To players of 30-button models: if you prefer, don't play the G sharp at all; play the preceeding A as a crotchet instead. You can use this trick in both these tunes.

Roxburgh Castle

Play Some Scottish Tunes

Peat Fire Flame

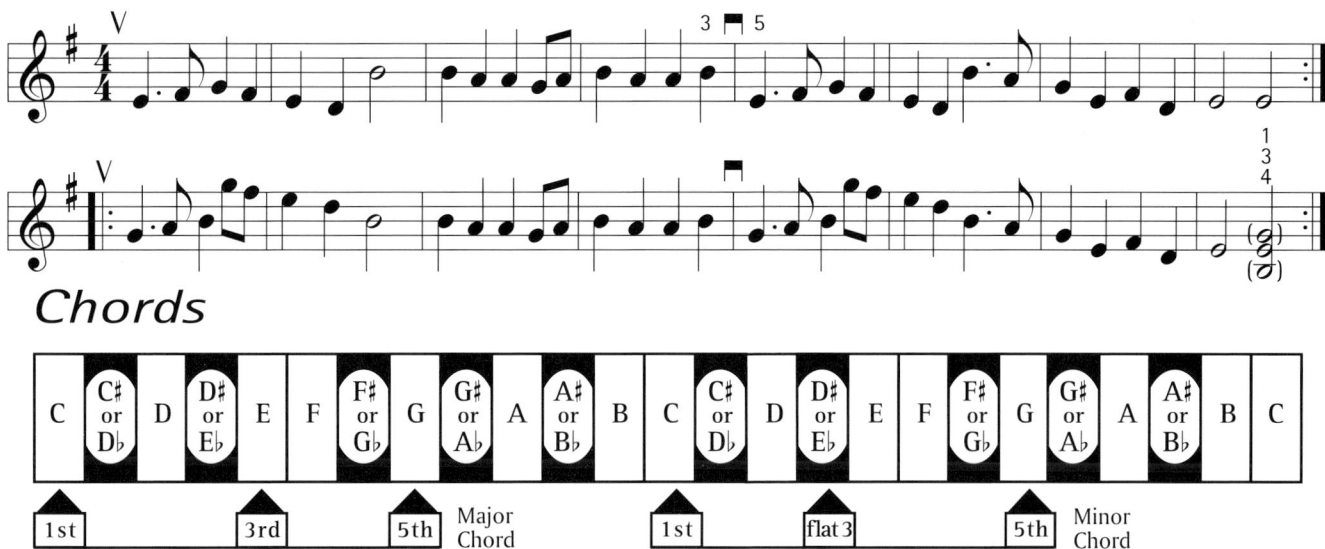

It's simple to find the notes of any major or minor chord using the musical ladder. All chords are based on the pattern **first** (known as the root), **third** and **fifth** notes of the major scale. Chords are named by their root note. Major chords consist of the **first**, **third** and **fifth** notes of the scale. Minor chords are **first**, **flattened third** and **fifth**. The notes of a chord can come in any order. If the **first** note (root note) is lowest the chord is said to be in the root position, if the **third** note is lowest it's in the first inversion, if **fifth** note is lowest it's in the second inversion. You can play chords on the English concertina by pressing several buttons at once. You can also play chords as a series of individual notes, these are known as arpeggios. You can find the notes of any chord by moving the sliders. For instance, the sliders in the positions above tell us that the notes of the chord of C major are C, E and G and the notes of C minor are C, E flat and G. The inversions are easiest to play because the notes occur on separate rows. You will find that the buttons are arranged in triangles when chords are played in the root position.

Rather than playing a single note to end a tune, it's nice to finish with a chord. Finish *Peat Fire Flame* with the chord of E minor second inversion, consisting of the notes B, E and G. On repeats, just play the E note. The first part of *Peat Fire Flame* is in E minor. The second part starts in the key of G major and only returns to E minor for the last two bars.

The Duke of Perth has its own dance. In bars 11 and 12, it's much simpler to use finger 2 twice rather than using the much more awkward 6 4 2 4 2 fingering. Facilitate this by playing the notes "staccato", meaning play them crisply, cut short and detached. Alternatively add a G 'slip note' and play 4 2 4 2 4 2.

Finish *Kate Dalrymple* with the chord of A major second inversion, consisting of the notes E, A and C sharp. On repeats, just play the A note.

Players of traditional music decorate tunes with various types of ornamentation and here in *Kate Dalrymple* we use an ornament called a "cut", a quick note running into the following main note. It is shown by the small G sharp note

continued overleaf

The English Concertina Absolute Beginners

29

Introducing Rants and Double Reels

Durham Rangers

immediately in front of the high A. This small note symbol is called a grace note. Grace notes have no time value of their own, they steal their time from the note they preceed. Making this cut is reasonably easy on standard models because the G sharp and the A are on different sides of the instrument. Players of 30-button instruments might consider this cut too awkward and prefer to leave it out.

Usually traditional music is played in medleys of two or three tunes. There are three such medleys on the soundtrack: *The Duke of Perth/Kate Dalrymple*, *Drowsy Maggie/Jack Broke da Prison Door* and *The Bush on the Hill/The Blackthorn Stick*.

Rants and reels are the same type of tune but rants are slightly less 'notey'. You might prefer to make more frequent bellows changes in these tunes. Rants, like *Durham Rangers*, are usually Northumbrian and are played for dances that involve the rant step. They're a bit easier to play than Irish double reels which are pretty much at the top of the degree of difficulty scale. *Durham Rangers*, also called *The Merry Sherwood Rangers*, is sometimes dotted like *Roxburgh Castle* and played as a hornpipe. Finish this tune with the chord of D major second inversion, consisting of the notes A, D and F sharp. On repeats, just play the D note.

Drowsy Maggie is an Irish reel in E minor dorian mode. Notice how in the A music, the melody keeps returning to the E note. This note is called the pivot note and is a very common feature in Irish reels. The A music can be quite tricky to play as long series of notes are all on one side and finger 1 has to alternate from second choice finger to first choice finger. *Jack Broke da Prison Door* is a fine reel from Shetland.

Drowsy Maggie

Jack Broke da Prison Door

Play Some Easy Melodies

Timmy O'Connor's Polka

In these last two pages, we'll play some tunes that include the less common notes. *Timmy O'Connor's Polka* is a brilliant Irish tune with three parts. The bar of music leading up to the A music really gives the tune a character of its own, and it's here that we get the chance to play the low A, low B and low C sharp notes. *The Ash Grove* is a very well-known, beautiful Welsh tune. It's a very old melody which has had numerous sets of lyrics, but to us tunesmiths, it's a lovely waltz. In this tune we find the low C natural. This note is also known as middle C because it occurs on a leger line between the treble and bass clefs in piano music. *Goodbye Girls I'm Going to Boston* is an American tune, excellent for the western squares. The B music has a recurring F natural accidental, and if we play it in two octaves, we get chance to play both the low and high F naturals. The alternating fingers technique really comes into its own in the B music making the notes sound clear and crisp. Finish *Goodbye Girls* with the chord of G major second inversion, consisting of the notes D, G and B. On repeats, just play the G note. Notice the D G B series at the beginning, play a B 'slip note' if necessary.

Below are several chords in their root positions to learn. Notice all the notes in each chord are on the same side and the three buttons form a triangle shape. There are always two notes, a fifth apart, which occur on the same row. You can press both these buttons with one finger (one-finger fifths) or use a different finger for each (two-finger fifths). Exactly how you finger these chords depends on the size of your hands, the previous notes and your personal preferences.

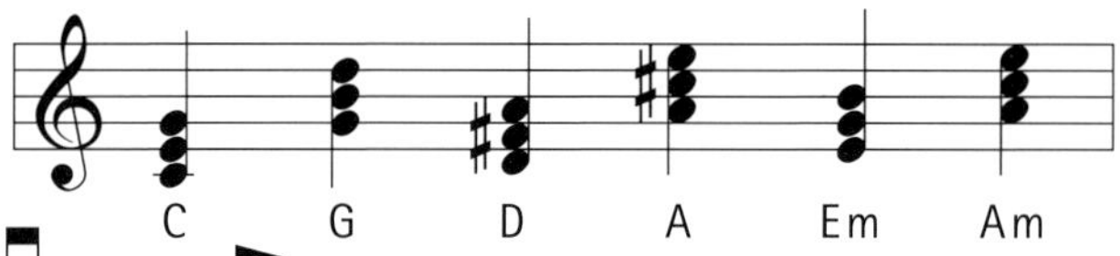

The Ash Grove

Goodbye Girls I'm Going to Boston

The English Concertina Absolute Beginners

31

Introducing Double Jigs

The Rambler

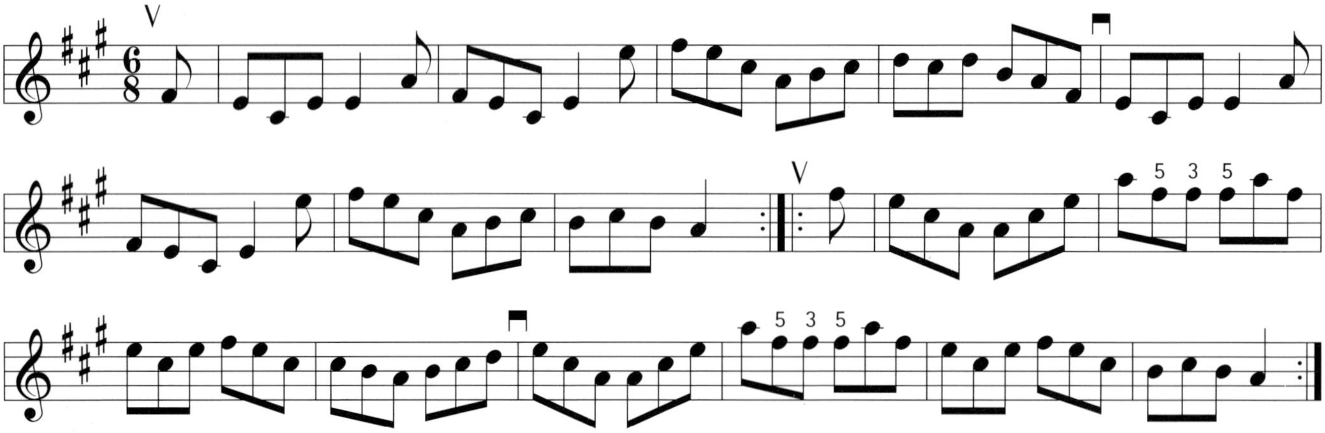

The Bush on the Hill

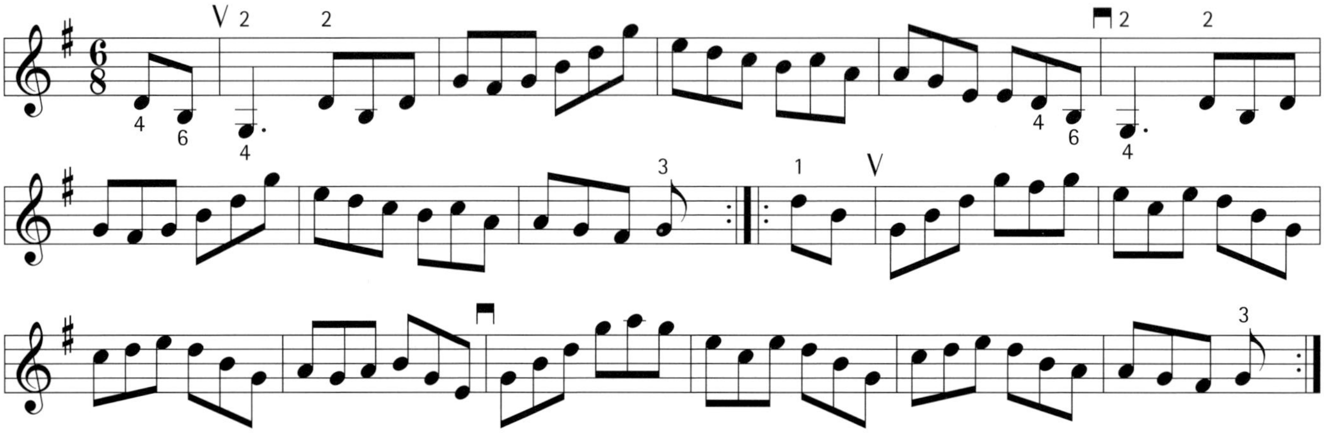

Irish music sessions are hugely popular, not only in Britain and Ireland, but all over the world. On this page we have three Irish double jigs often heard in such sessions. Double jigs have a predominance of groups of three quavers.

The Rambler is in the key of A but has no G sharp. It's a great tune and features the low C sharp. The alternating finger technique is really useful in the B music. *The Bush on the Hill* goes down to the low G, the lowest note of traditional music and the lowest note of the fiddle. It isn't convenient to use our second choice finger 4 to play the low G note because we want it to play the preceeding B note. However, this doesn't worry us because the low G note is a dotted crotchet, giving us the opportunity to steal a 'quavers-worth of time' so we can use the same finger to play the following D note. Alternatively use the fingering shown under the stave. In Irish sessions *The Blackthorn Stick* is usually played in the key of G but often Scottish ceilidh bands tend to favour the key of A. This is a very popular tune, well-known to players of English, Irish and Scottish music. The tune is widely used for rapper sword dancing. The format of the last bar of each part is a typical feature of double jigs. Use the 1 3 1 alternating fingers technique to play the last three notes. 'Steal a quaver' from the last G note in order to use finger 1 again to play the pick-up note D. Alternatively use a B 'slip note'. Make sure your thumbs are not too far through the straps or you might have difficulty reaching the low notes featured in these last two pages.

Well! That's it! Time now to really start learning the English concertina. It's up to you to create your own style. You're on your own now. Good luck. See you at a session somewhere.

The Blackthorn Stick

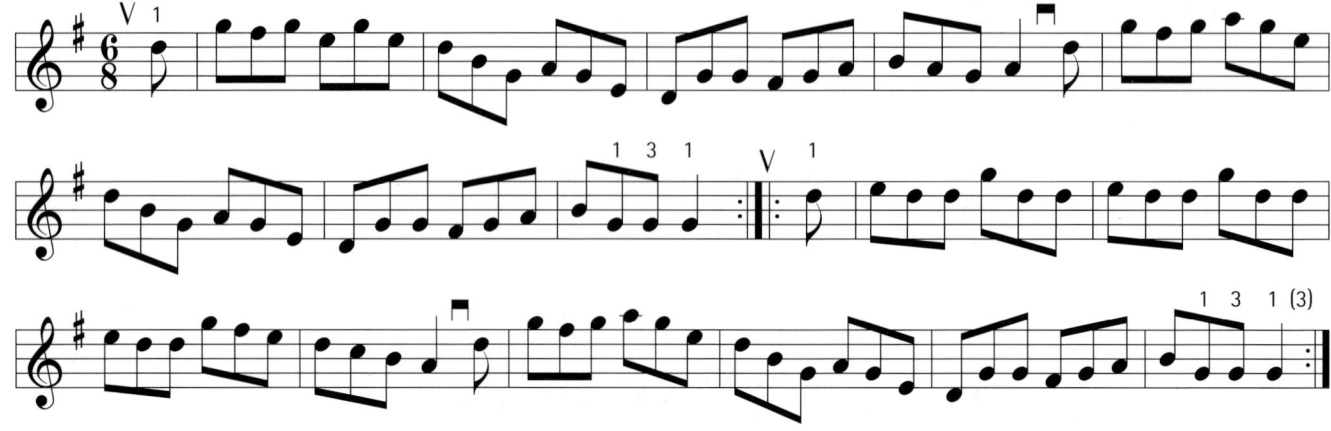